To :-

From :-

Other mini books in the series
To a very Special Daughter
To a very Special Friend
To a very Special Grandmother
To my very Special Husband
To my very Special Love
To a very Special Mother
Happy Anniversary

Published in the USA in 1992 by Exley Giftbooks
Published in Great Britain in 1992 by Exley Publications Ltd
Reprinted 1993
Third printing 1993
Fourth printing 1994

Illustrations copyright © Helen Exley 1992
Selection copyright © Helen Exley 1992

ISBN 1-85015-323-X

A copy of the CIP data is available from the British Library on request.

Illustrations by Juliette Clarke
Written by Pam Brown
Edited by Helen Exley.

Printed and bound in Hungary.

Dedication:
For Tracey Salter, wishing you every happiness, with love from Juliette.

Exley Publications Ltd., 16 Chalk Hill, Watford, Herts WD1 4BN,
United Kingdom.
Exley Giftbooks, 232 Madison Avenue, Suite 1206, NY 10016, USA.

Wishing you
HAPPINESS

Written by Pam Brown
Illustrations by Juliette Clarke

<u>I WISH YOU</u>

- adventures with happy endings.

- mornings of glad anticipation.

- quiet sleep and glad awakening.

. . .

EXLEY
NEW YORK • WATFORD, UK

<u>MY WISHES FOR YOU</u>

I wish you the joy of always having someone to
share things with.

· · ·

My wish for you is that sometimes, just sometimes,
you can afford the thing you long for, rather than
the thing that will do.

· · ·

I wish you enough good memories to see you through the bad times.

. . .

I wish you one of the best of small happinesses, the opening of a well-remembered book, the smoothing of the page, the first familiar words...

. . .

I wish you the happiness of finding the perfect present for someone you love.

. . .

I wish you spring - the amazement that is always better than you dared expect.

. . .

I wish you the happiness of a gift from a child;
- a bunch of wilting dandelions
- a fluff-coated toffee
- a frog
- a kiss

. . .

NATURE'S GIFTS

May you, just once or twice in your lifetime,
see something infinitely rare and strange
and beautiful.

. . .

I wish you the delight of plants - the small miracles
of graft and cutting, seed and bulb and corm. Of
new life from the earth.

. . .

I wish you the gloom of the garden in winter
- and, after months of anticipation,
the small, green signs of Spring.

. . .

I wish you a fascination for the infinite variety
of animal life...

Who could have imagined elephants?

Giraffes? The platypus?

Who would have suspected the kaleidoscope of lives
beneath the sea?

Or golden eagles, sprawled upon the wind.

Or silver-whiskered mice. Or turquoise damselflies.

We share our world with a million, million lives.

Wonders.

The hunch and reach of cats. The leap of gazelles.

The sinuous strength of slowworms.

The jauntiness of foxes.

Not slaves or servants to human beings.

Companions, worthy of respect.

· · ·

I wish you the trust of
a wild creature - won
with patience and love.

MAY YOU ALWAYS...

... get the front door open and charge to the
phone before it stops ringing.

... say the right thing to the wine waiter.

... remember your zipper.

... have enough money to get home.

... be necessary to someone.

... find a useful coin in the
lining of your pocket.

... be astonished by your own abilities.

... find that the grim brown envelope turns
out to contain a receipt.

... fall in love with reality and not illusion.

... find exactly the right retort - succinct,
memorable, overwhelming - at the time and
not half an hour later.

<u>MAY YOU NEVER...</u>

... miss that last mail collection.

... start to applaud at the end of the
second movement.

... lose track of which cutlery you are
supposed to be using.

... find that the concert you had tickets for was
yesterday.

... turn up to a posh do in shoes that
don't match.

... lose your credit card.

... have a television that goes phutt at the
crucial moment.

... get given a pot plant that breathes its last the
day before your friend's visit.

... leave the shopping list on the kitchen table.

STRENGTH AND COURAGE

If I had the power to make one wish for you, I would find it very hard to decide what gift to give - what gift would help you to happiness. Beauty is dangerous, wisdom must be earned, love is of your own choosing.

But in the end, I am certain that I would choose the best gift of all - and that is courage.

. . .

May you never purchase "love" at the price of becoming a doormat.

. . .

May you always find exactly the right words to put bullies in their place - and enough strength in your knees to walk out with dignity.

. . .

May you have a loving heart - and shrewd judgment.

. . .

There is great happiness
to be found in giving.
But giving endlessly
can drain the mind and
heart. Learn to take a little
- even if it is a moment in
the garden, a gallery, a café.
Appreciate it.
Let birds and frogs and
pictures, music and books
and undemanding friends
restore you.
People need nourishment.

. . .

I WISH YOU THE JOY OF:

Seeing your luggage come safely round the carousel.

A letter from someone whose address you have lost.

Seeing someone's face light up at the sight of you.

Knowing you are needed.

Finding the perfect present.

The car starting first go when the prospective
buyer tries it.

Spotting your missing cat plodding up the path

The smell of land, far out to sea

A skein of geese passing low overhead, calling

Biplanes stunting on a summer's day

Sun-dried linen

Donkeys

Dawn, mid ocean

The right one realizing just who you really are

inside - and loving you for it.

Taking off your smart shoes

The sight of the one you love at the end

of the platform

Pistachio nuts

Renoir

Discovering that you have not, after all, thrown

your friend's letter on the fire with the

birthday wrappings

Walking in the rain

Pigs

. . .

If I could, I would spare you all the heart sinking
moments when Happiness Goes Wrong.
<u>I **DON'T** WISH YOU . . .</u>

- The cake that emerges, golden and domed - and
deflates as you watch.

- The rare bird in a distant tree that turns out -
under the eye of the binoculars - to be a piece
of tatty rag.

- The awaited phone call that's a wrong number.

- The envelope that reveals you've won a month in the Caribbean - but on a second reading dwindles into a cruel advertising gimmick for Timeshare.
- The face that lights up at the sight of you, but passes by to someone just behind.
- The shining in the gutter that prodding reveals to be a ring pull.
- The designer label sweater in the garage sale that proves to have a crimson paint stain on the back.
- The perfect sale shoes half a size too small.
- The seeds that flourish - and turn out to be weeds.
- The expensively-packaged scent that smells like an unwashed dog.
- The bouquet of daffodils that rot in the bud.
- The TV show you sit up till midnight to see - only to find you've seen it before.
- The film of the picnic that comes back blank.
- The wrongly-delivered parcel.
- The mutual love that turns out not to be.

. . .

I wish you the happiness of love, that does not change with change, that shines as surely in age as in youth.

FRIENDS

I hope you always have room in your life

for another friend.

. . .

I wish you letters:

in handwriting that you recognize at once;

in handwriting that you have not seen for years;

in handwriting totally unknown.

I wish you letters full of praise,

full of encouragement;

letters of thanks and love.

I wish you letters of apology from manufacturers

- with unexpected prizes

I wish you letters that begin

"We are glad to tell you that..."

I wish you letters with foreign stamps

and exciting letterheads

I wish you grubby, inky, crooked-written letters,

covered with cross-kisses.

. . .

IN TIMES OF TROUBLE...

Analyzing the causes of anguish is effort wasted. There is no going back. No spell can change what has happened, no blaming this or that. Whenever you're deeply troubled, persuade your mind to concentrate on little, present pleasures. Give yourself time to heal. Be still.

. . .

Loss leaves us empty - but learn not to close your heart and mind in grief. Allow life to replenish you. When sorrow comes it seems impossible - but new joys wait to fill the void.

. . .

I wish you the happiness of letting the past go - and finding new beginnings.

I wish I could save you from every
sorrow, every disaster, every failure.
But then you would be cut off from
all other creatures on the planet. It is
our heartache as much as our
happiness that makes a family or a
marriage, or a friendship.

. . .

If I could give you anything it would
be a quietness at the very heart of
your life that would remain tranquil
and certain whatever befell.

. . .

Hold happiness gently.
It is on loan.

. . .

I WISH YOU THE JOY OF WATER

Slow river; shallow silent stream.

Bubble of a spring through clumps of violets.

Chatter of woodland brook.

Roar of cataract.

The spurt of a garden hose.

The dazzle of fountains.

The sheen of water sliding over stone.

Puddles stuck with crimson leaves.

Waves solid as green glass, leaving their foam

to ride the swell.

The chattering of water past a racing hull.

Small rainbows in the morning spiderwebs.

Dew on bare feet.

Frog faces in a pool.

Lakes holding summer skies.

Rain battering the window of your

own safe home.

. . .

... THE COMING OF SPRING

Hyacinths shove their shining snouts through
the bare earth
and buds break out of the naked branches.
Can you smell the air?
This is the astonishment called spring.
This is the thaw
when your dull winter breaks in a rush of joy
- and you are always young.

Here are the veins of
your hand. Here
streams run to meet
the river. We are bound
together. The same life
flows through all
things. Be happy in this
unity, this continuity.

. . .

DISCOVERY!

I wish you the joy of "I *see!* I understand!!"

. . .

I wish you the happiness of ideas, the excitement of
reason, the triumph of understanding, the clearing
of sight, the sharpening of hearing, the reaching
out to new discovery, a pleasure in the past
as well as in the present.
I wish you the joy of creativity.

. . .

I wish you the joy of mastery - of your own muscles,
of a boat, of a bike, of a horse, of paint and canvas,
plain and purl, pastry, engines, calculus or French.
Anything. Everything.

. . .

May there always, always be something you
want to learn, something you want to do,
somewhere you want to go, someone you
want to meet. May life never grow stale.

. . .

Happiness is a quiet,
perpetual rejoicing
in small events.

LITTLE THINGS

Happiness comes in a million forms - like art.
We need the great and memorable
- enduring love, friendship,
achievement, music and discovery.
But we need the small and silly too:
Laurel and Hardy, rain on the window, cats in the
bed, mushrooms in the grass, double rainbows, the
fading of house lights and the sigh of a rising
curtain, home-baked bread.
And moonlight on meadows, a long-sought book
discovered, stars, the dentist's "Nothing to be done".
All things that lift the heart and make the dullest
day worth living.

Be happy in small things.
They give great happinesses
the opportunity to creep up
on you, quietly.

. . .

I wish you small delights - designer labels peering
out from piles of tat at garage sales, seeds that
take and sprout and flourish, double yolks, a robin
in the apple tree, coins in the gutter, an elephant
hawk moth caterpillar in the brushwood,
a scarey ride on a roller coaster, a small sticky kiss,
a cat on a wall that needs its belly rubbed,
a passing biplane flinging itself into a
loop-the-loop. A squirrel in your tree. An
unexpected parcel. The train on time.

. . .

I wish you small unexpected happinesses - an
invitation, a gift, a smile from a stranger.

. . .

WHEREVER YOU GO

There will be new beginnings as you move

off the old, familiar, well-trodden path.

There will be difficulties you never dreamed

of, moments of doubt, moments of fear

- but there will be amazements too. A turn

in the path - and the world will be at your

feet, another and you will be passing through a

wooded ravine.

All along your way there will be new things

to see and taste and smell and touch.

This will be the way you choose.

This will be your happiness, your life.

My thoughts go with you.

. . .

Friends are not always there to help good things
happen. But even if you are alone with your camel
in the middle of the Sahara, or steering single-
handed through a South Atlantic gale - their
thoughts are with you and their wishes for
wonderful things to happen. Think of your friends
as you check your compass or shorten sail. They
want you to find the special happiness you seek.

. . .

I wish you happiness
but not the happiness which is purchased
by shutting out the world.
Nor that of denying your dream for comfort's sake.
I wish you the happiness of doing what you do
as best you can.
Of taking the risk of trying
of taking the risk of giving
of taking the risk of loving.

. . .